France-Lise & Rita McGurn

MATCHING MOTHER/DAUGHTER TATTOOS

Text by Neil Clements
Published by Margot Samel & Lugemik

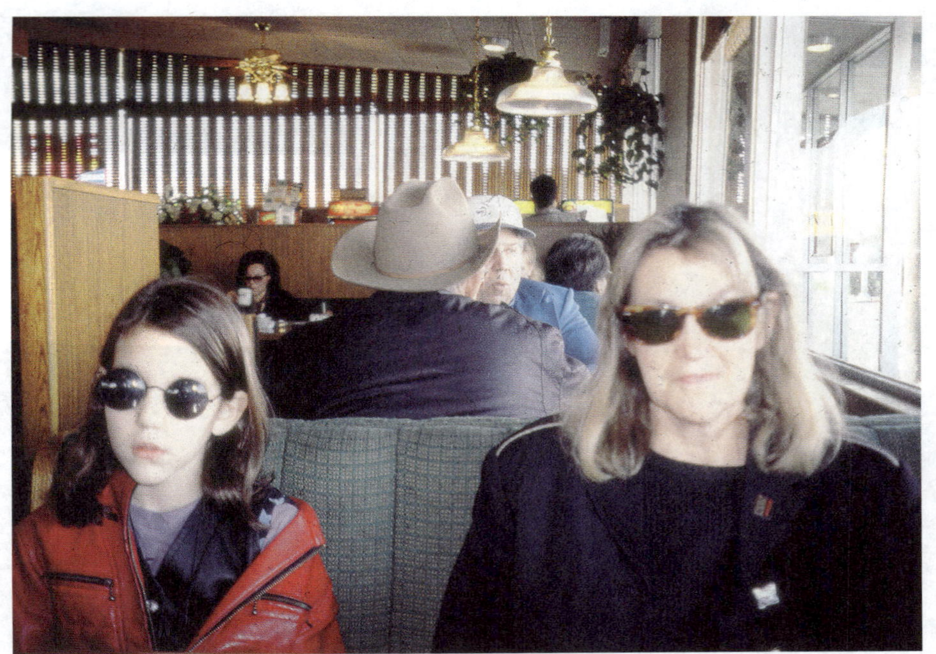

France-Lise and Rita McGurn. Glasgow. 1980s

> The story was, me returning home from a trip to NY and showing her my new black star tattoo I got to match hers. She was busy cooking, as per, and turned to me with an eyebrow raised. In her kinda cutting sarcasm she said 'matching mother daughter tattoos? Charming.' She was half smiling and DEEPLY unimpressed.

In spite of the warmth and succour that they provide, familial relationships are not without a degree of complexity. Nor should any account of them become so reductive as to obscure that. A defining paradox of any feminist approach is the necessity to speak both on behalf of a collectively disenfranchised group, and yet as an individual. This is no less true of the social bonds that tie mothers so fundamentally to their daughters. Two matching tattoos depicting a black star, one inked in the backroom of a bar in Perpignan in 1998, another applied in New York five years later, stand here as a symbol of this inherent tension: the desire to belong, and to all the while establish some form of autonomy.

Outside of an eclectic career working between interior design, theatre and television, Rita McGurn maintained an artistic practice from the 1970s onwards, creating a substantial body of artworks that would seldom be exhibited in her lifetime. Her daughter France-Lise grew up in a domestic environment that prominently featured these artworks, and this formed an ever-changing backdrop for the development of her own practice as a painter. Subsequent to her mother's passing in 2015, France-Lise has acted as one of the principal custodians of this work, housing an archive her drawings and crocheted sculptures in her own studio.

To preserve the estate of a family member, so as to communicate the value of objects that have contributed so much to one's own visual understanding of the world, is a profound gesture of care. It is also a significant responsibility to assume. Rita McGurn was neither in the habit of titling or dating the artworks she compulsively produced, preferring to instead regard them as elements of a continuously unfolding, endlessly alterable tapestry, one that was directly overlaid on the life she led. As such, any subsequent display of this material offers only a partial glimpse of what was a monumental undertaking, its retrospective compartmentalisation as exhibitions being an inherently subjective endeavour.

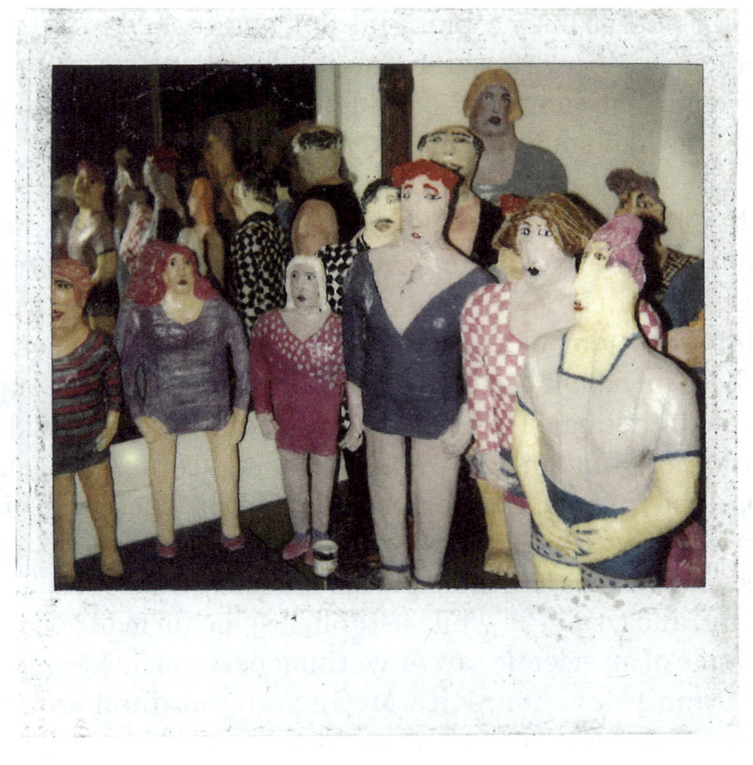

Rita McGurn's papier-mâché sculptures, Glasgow, 1980s

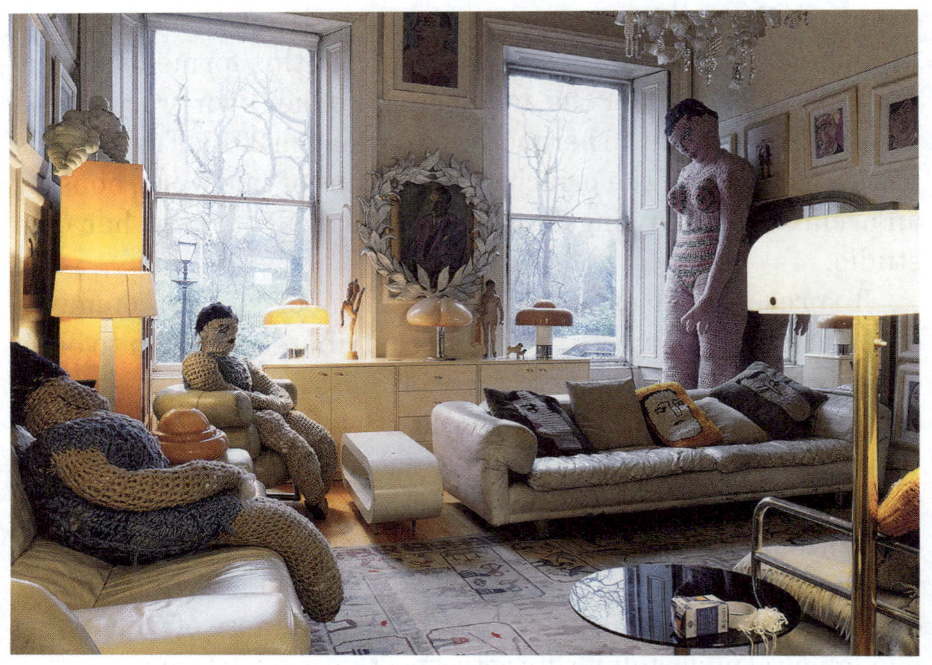

Rita and Peter McGurn's living room, Glasgow, 2021

Beyond their common foundation in figurative representation there are several points of aesthetic departure that distinguish these two practices. The gallus spirit of the self-trained mother, who attended art school not as a student but as a life model, operates on a different register to the Apollonian elegance cultivated by the daughter, a grace that has been honed on an international stage. After all, these are two practices diametrically opposed in terms of the context they operate in. One was carried out for largely personal edification, and that of family and a close circle of friends. The other now continuously circulates, evolving under the gaze of a much less differentiated audience.

Both constitute freedoms of a kind—freedom from unwanted oversight, the freedom that mobility affords—while being circumscribed by other factors. Their combination might offer some insight into an ideal set of artistic conditions, a space that is at once private and yet porously public, alternating between shelter and arena, as and when required. In reality, these positions are far more likely to be regarded as the constituent elements of a zero-sum relationship, visibility inevitably coming with attendant expectations; the products of seclusion carrying inside themselves a particular flavour of entropic sadness. Combined perhaps, these two practices form an antidote to such thinking, a model for a way of being that has yet to come to be.

If a shared premise is to be found in the respective practices of Rita and France-Lise McGurn, it would be better located in an attitude towards the boundaries between creative activity and the aspects of everyday life that surround it. This is an impulse to expand beyond established confines, to figure an exuberance that cannot be contained. In both of their artworks we encounter characters absorbed in the rituals of life, but these are less depictions of specific individuals than they are depictions of the fabric of sociality itself. Touchstones for this sense of restless movement—be it Glasgow's Barras Market during the 1980s, or its Sub-Club of the early noughts—are converted into universalised representations of collective congregation. The crowds that each construct are alternate families, ones that exist in parallel to a biological family. They are metaphorical representations of the company that we both desire and chafe against.

— Neil Clements

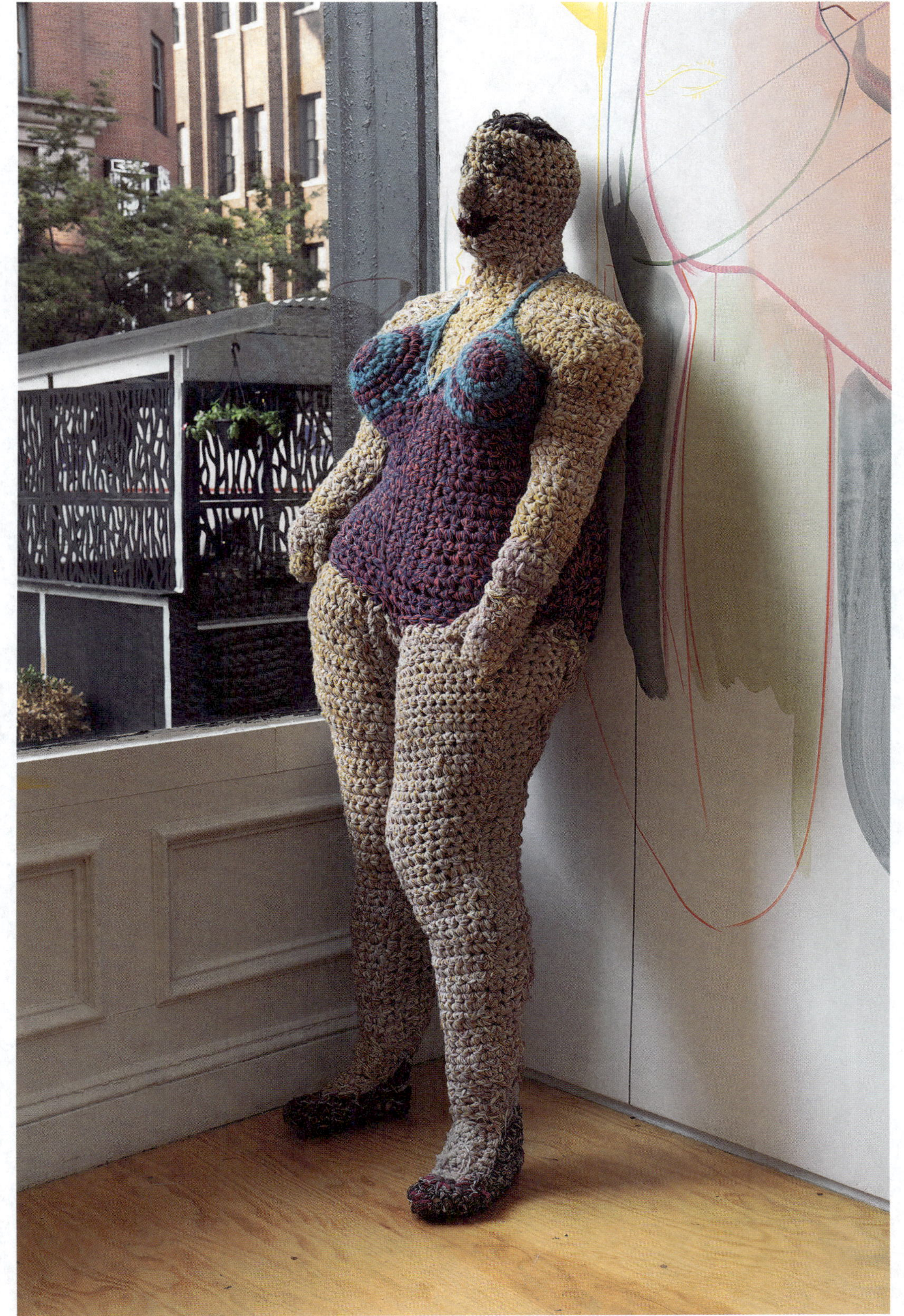

Rita McGurn. Untitled, 2000–2010

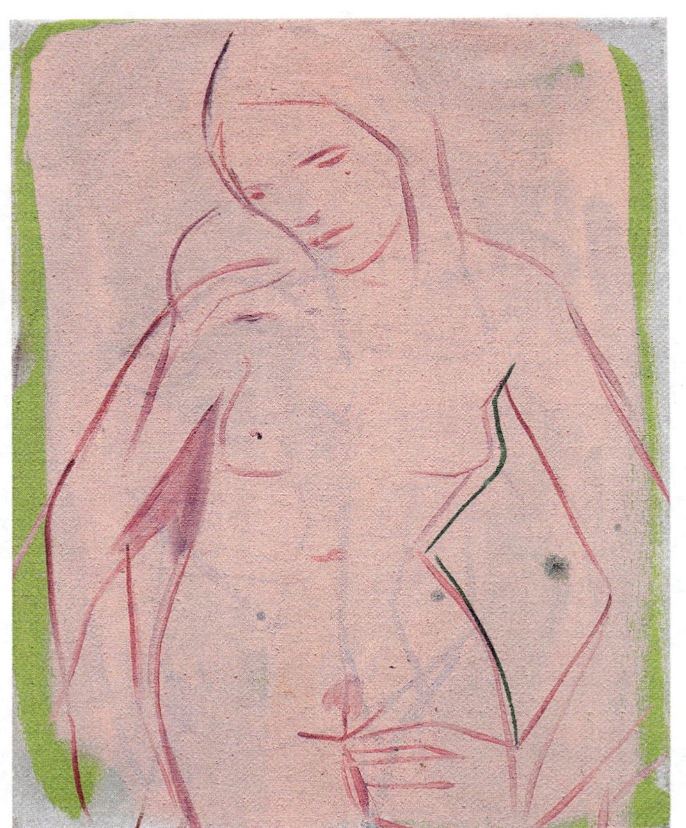

France-Lise McGurn. Momfluencer, 2023

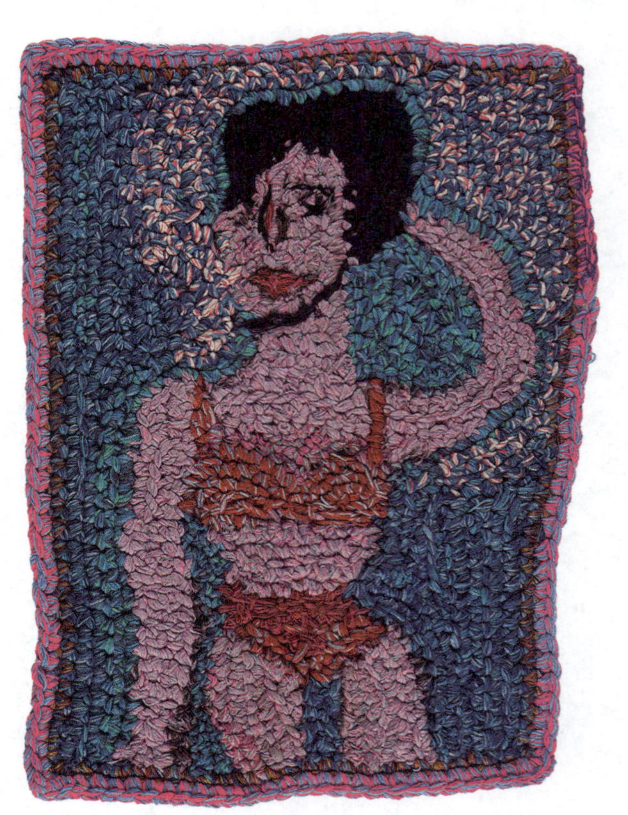

Rita McGurn. Untitled, 1990–2010

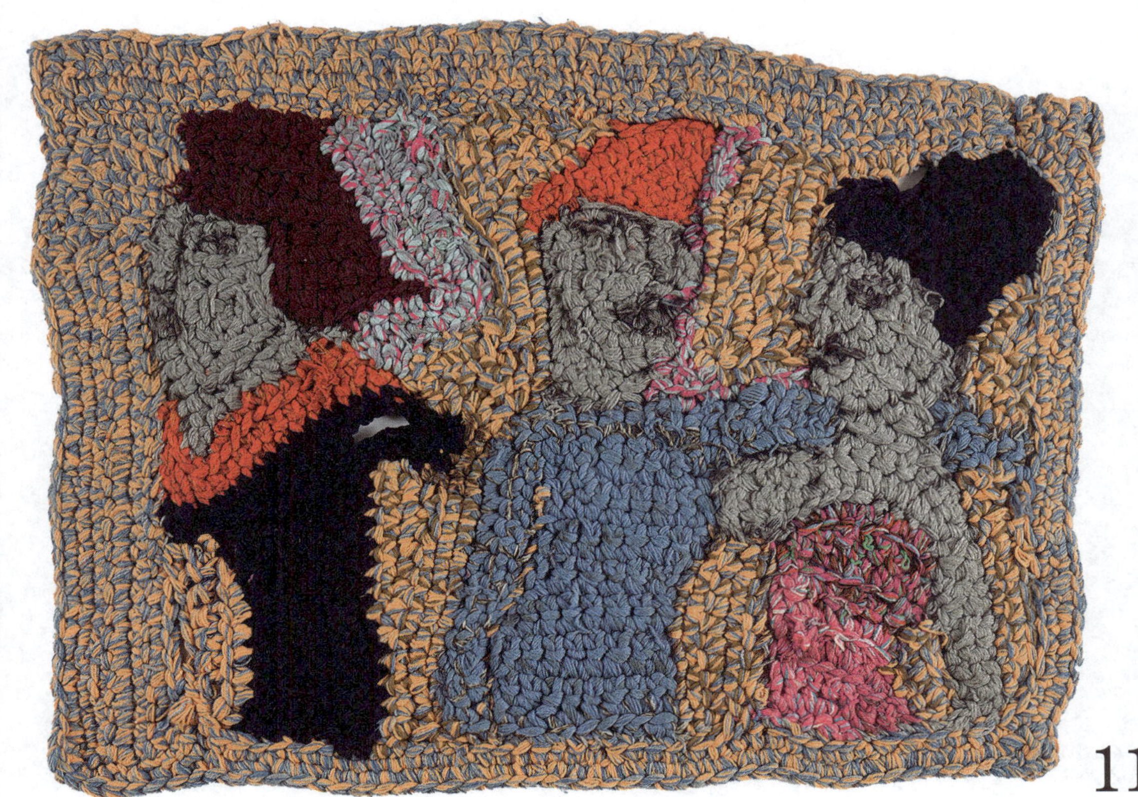

Rita McGurn. Untitled, 1990–2010

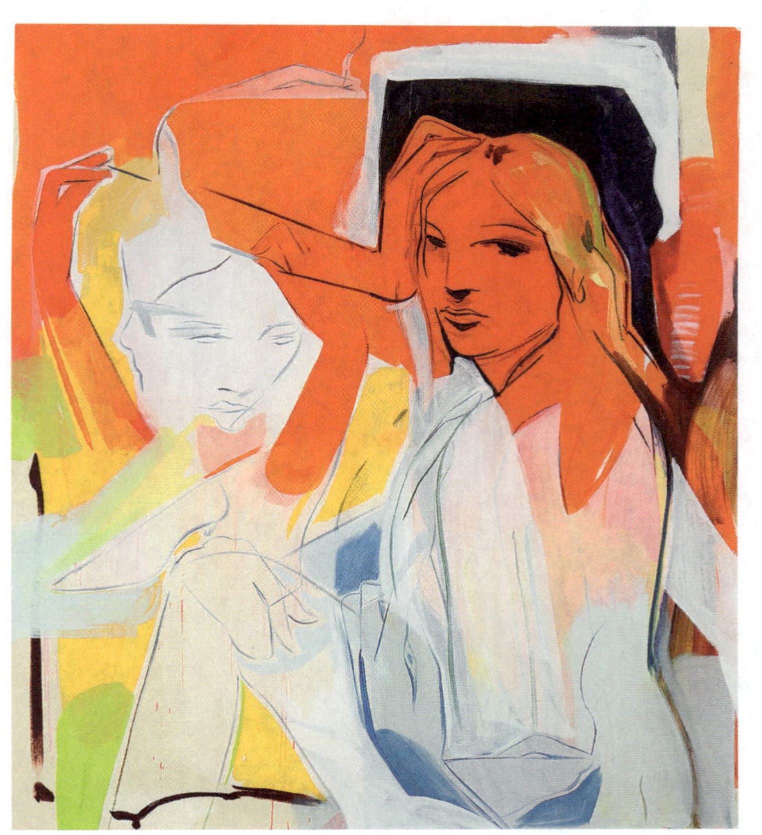

France-Lise McGurn. 90s mirror, 2023

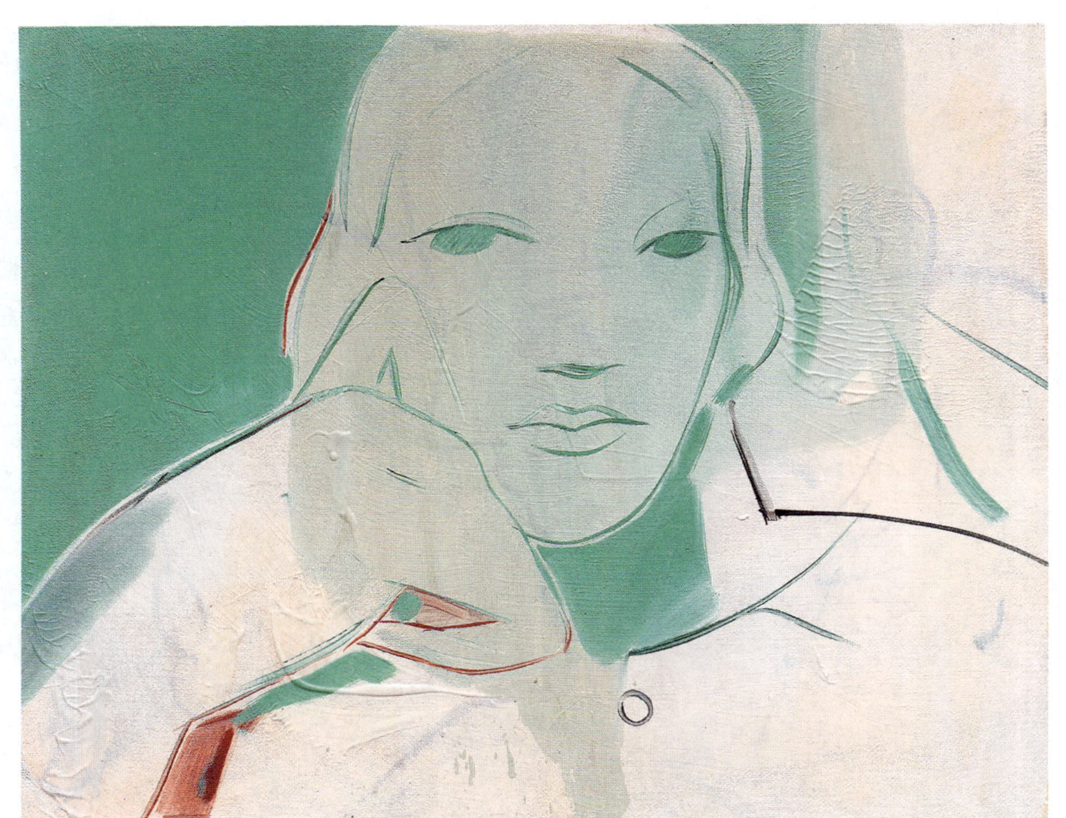

France-Lise McGurn. Piece peace, 2023

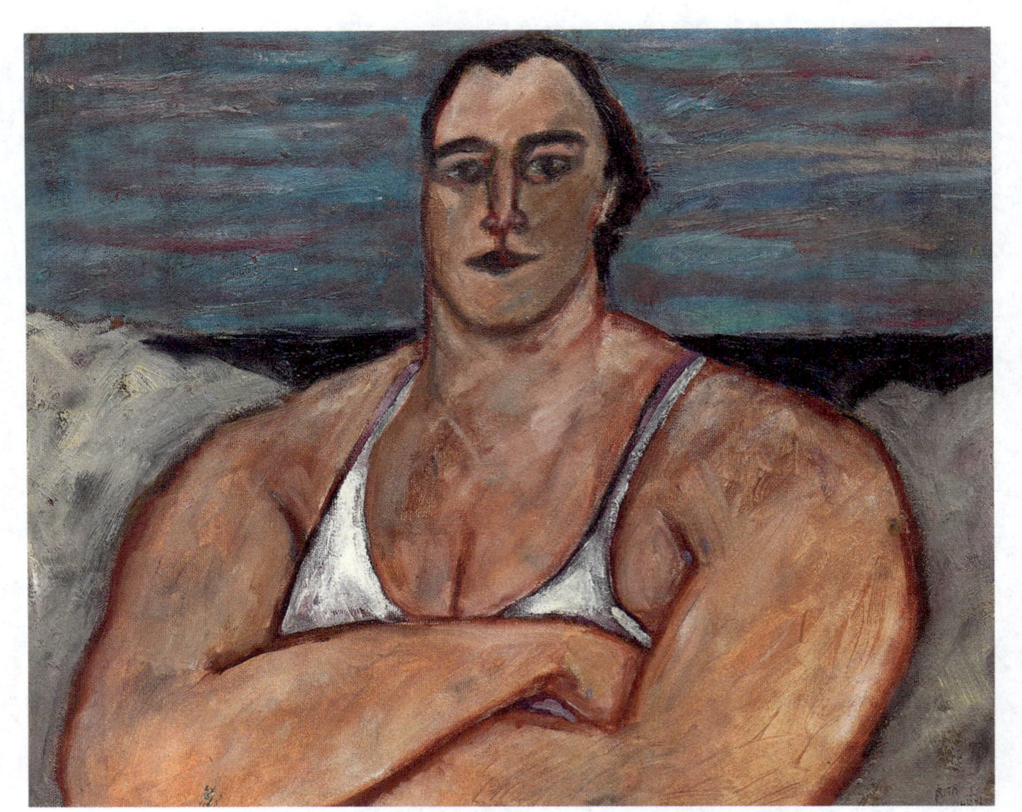

Rita McGurn. Untitled, 1990–1999

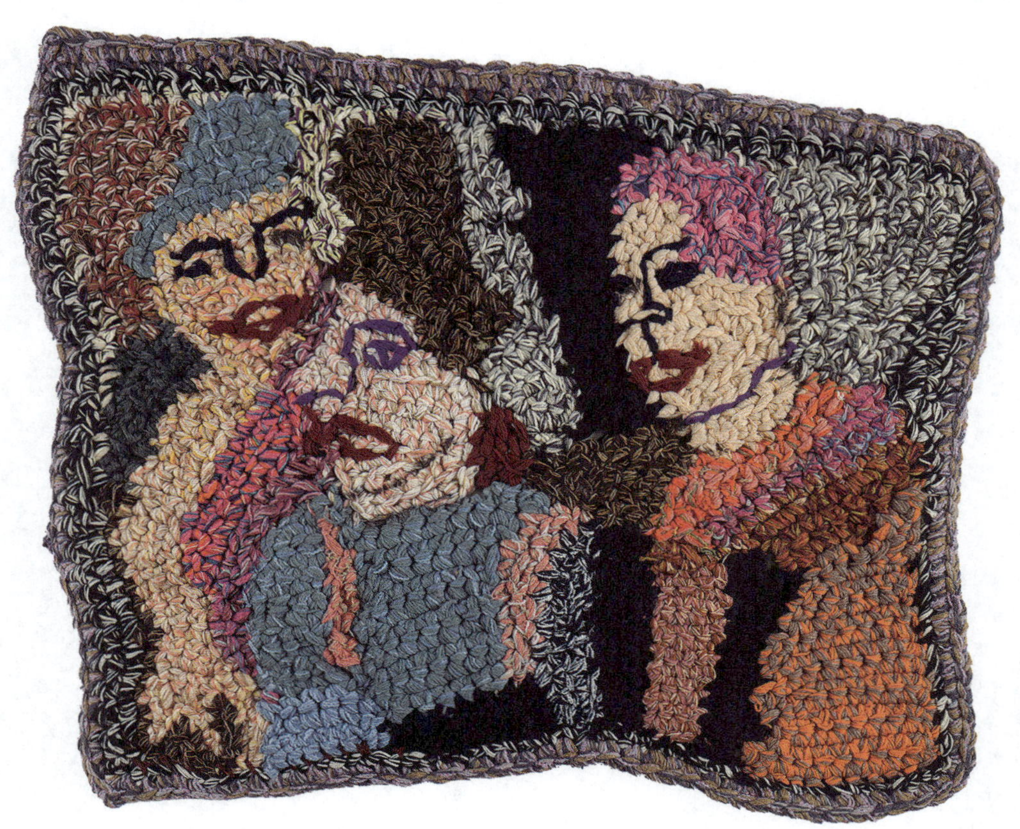

Rita McGurn. Untitled, 1990–2010

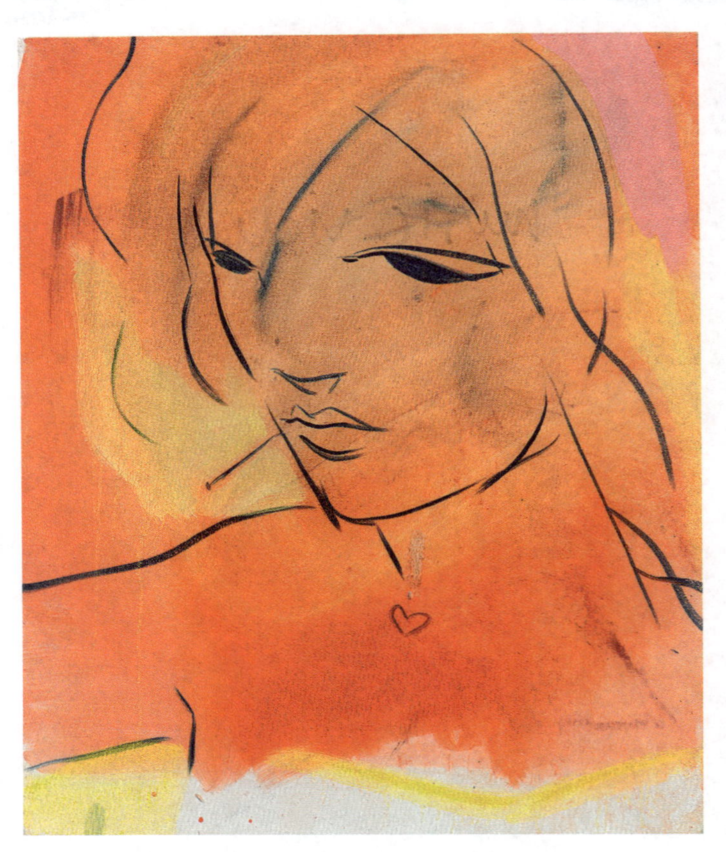

France-Lise McGurn. Music video, 2023

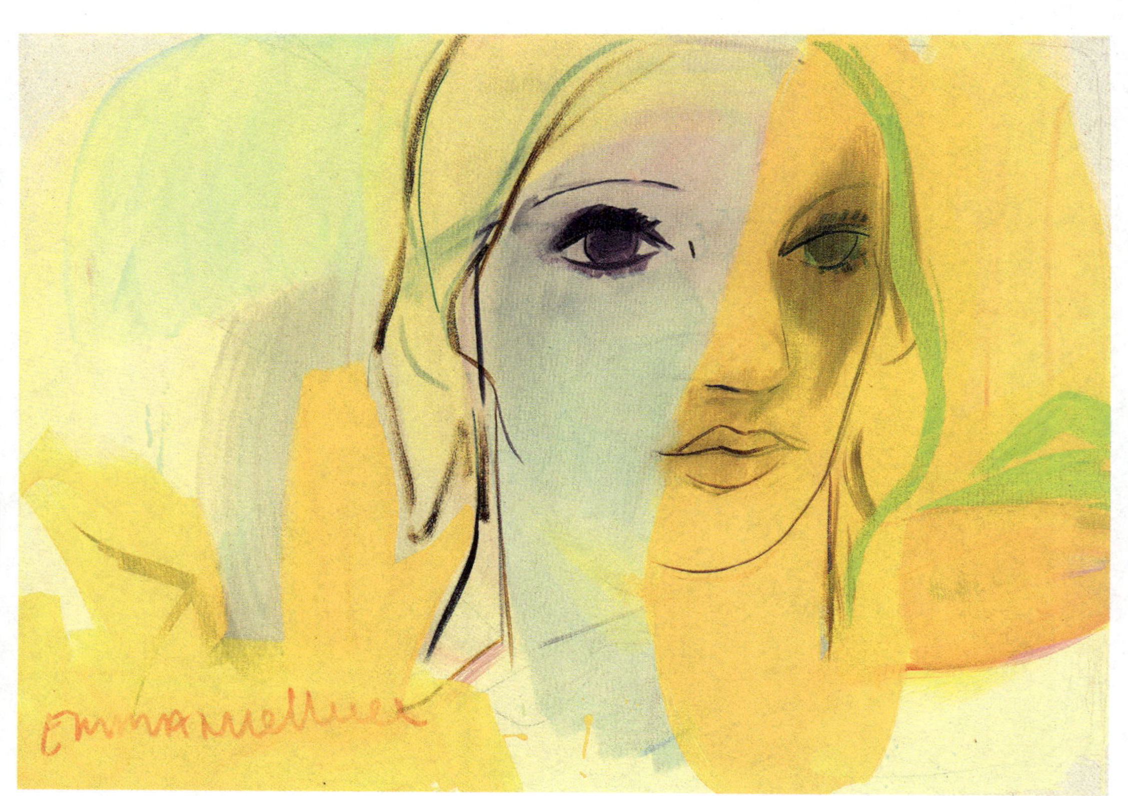

France-Lise McGurn. Sinéad, 2023

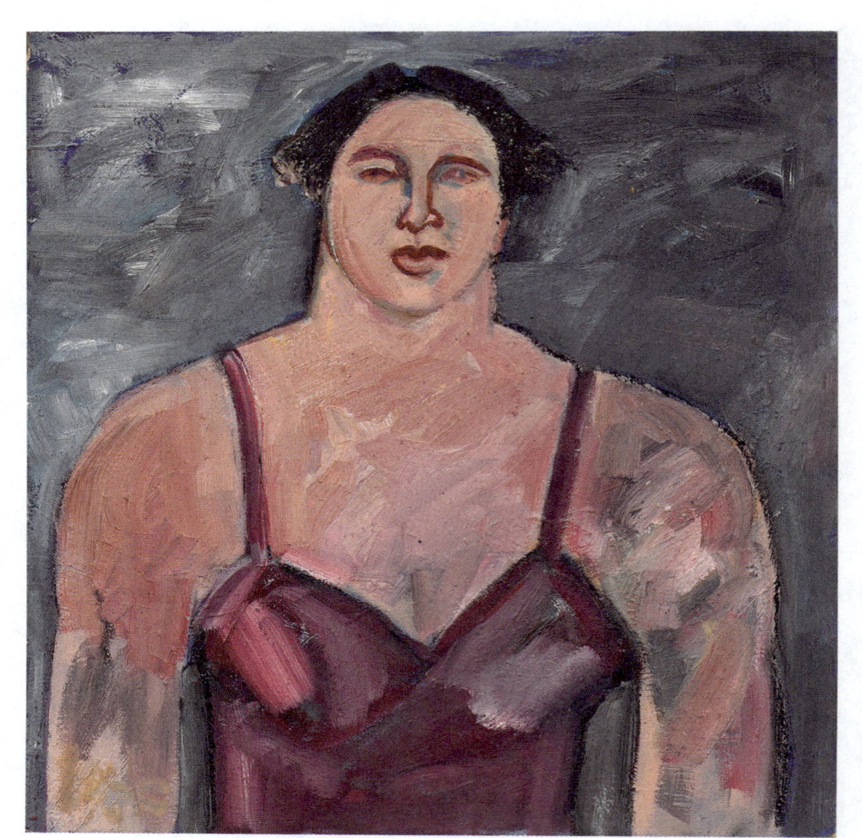

Rita McGurn. Untitled, 1990–1999

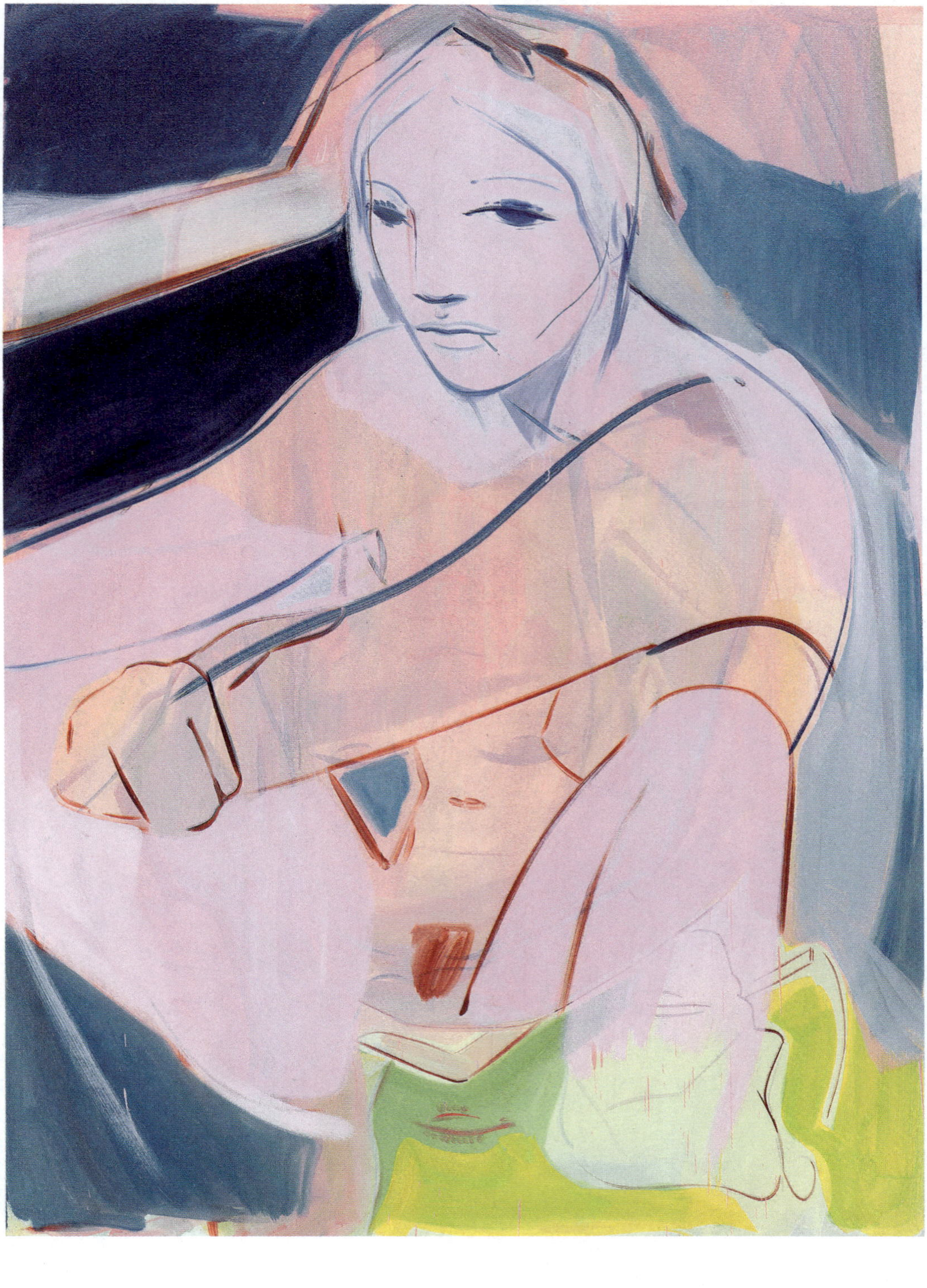

France-Lise McGurn. Zoflora, the midnight blooms, 2023

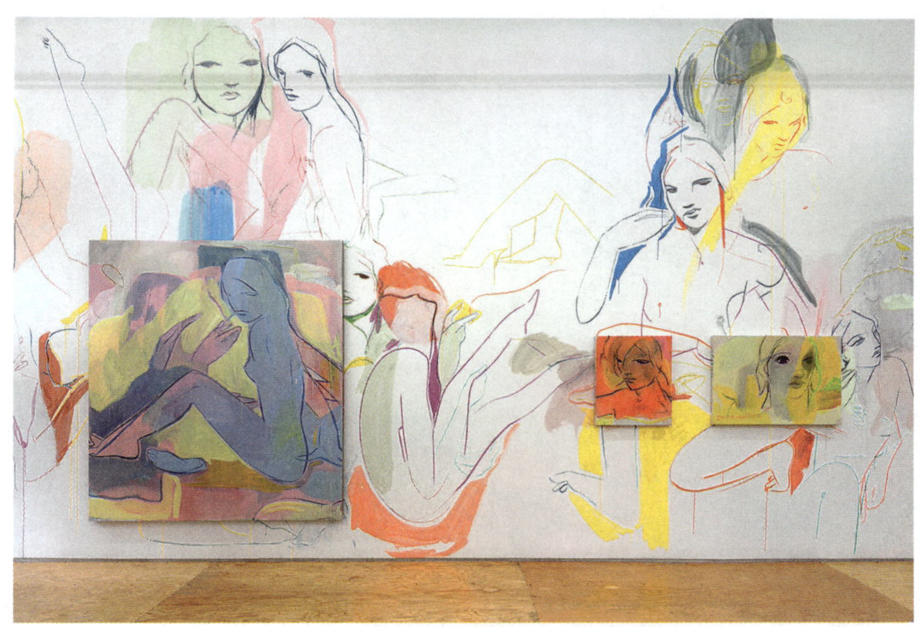

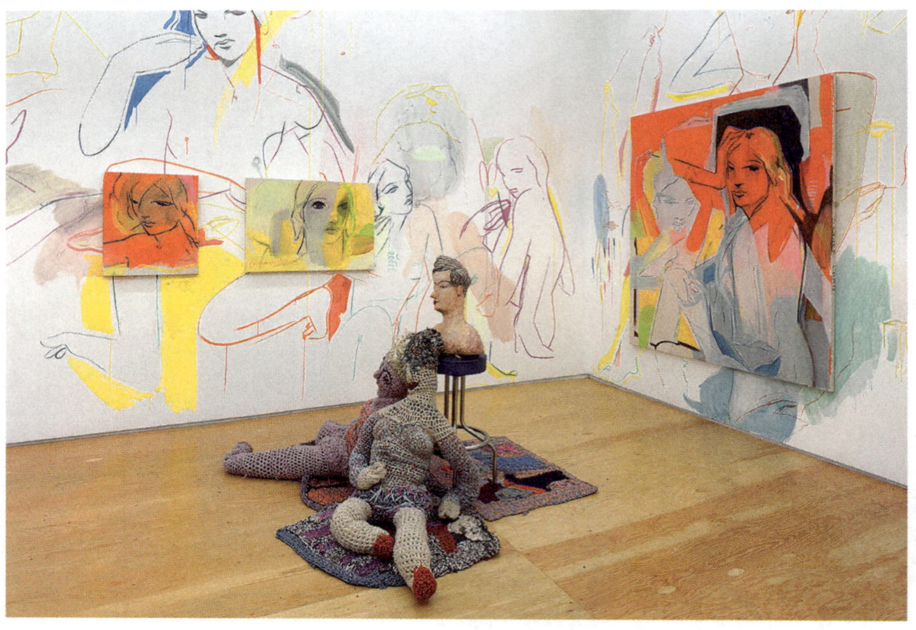

France-Lise McGurn and Rita McGurn. Matching Mother/Daughter Tattoos.
Exhibition views at Margot Samel, New York, September 2023.

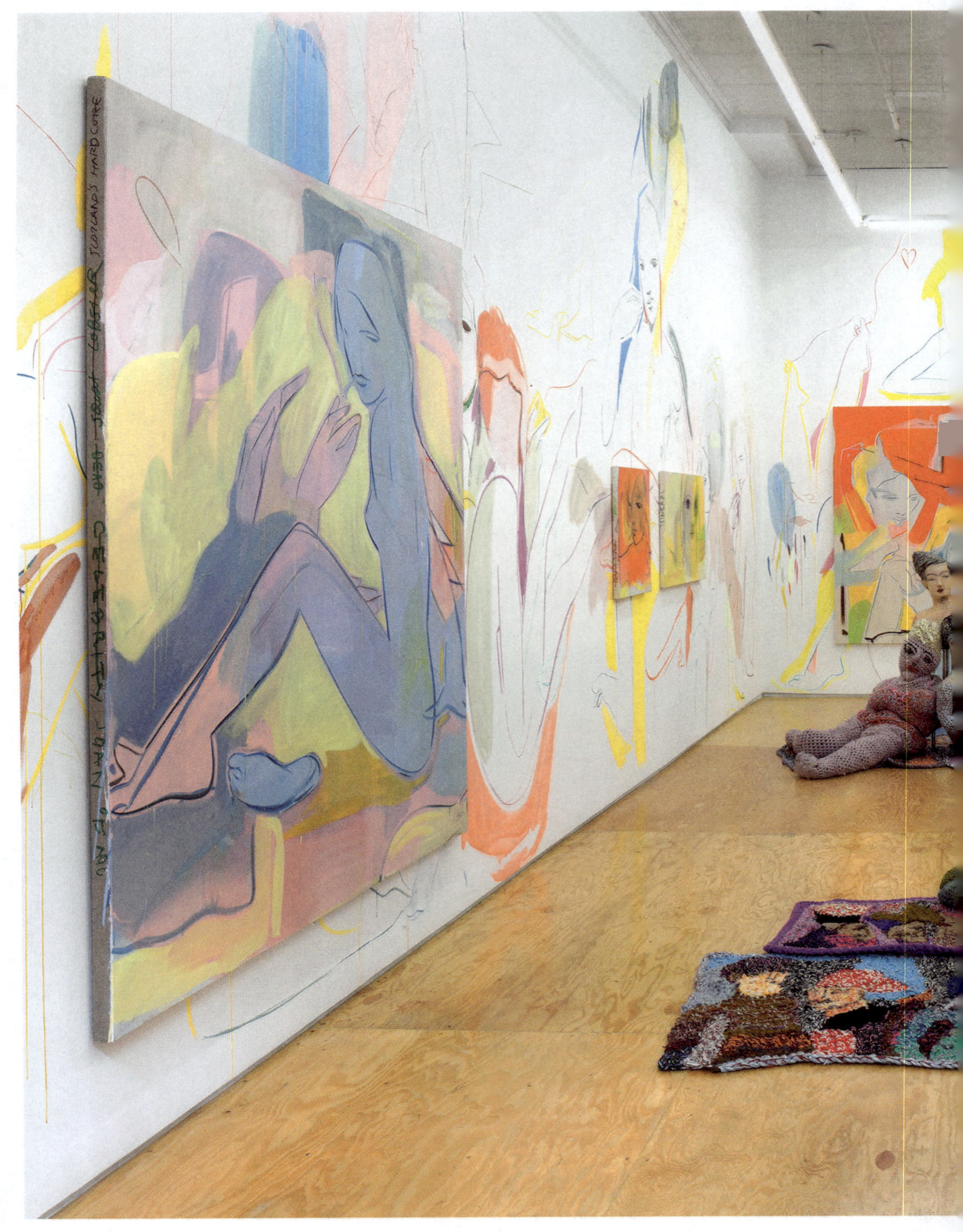

France-Lise McGurn and Rita McGurn. Matching Mother/Daughter Tattoos. Exhibition view at Margot Samel, New York, September 2023.

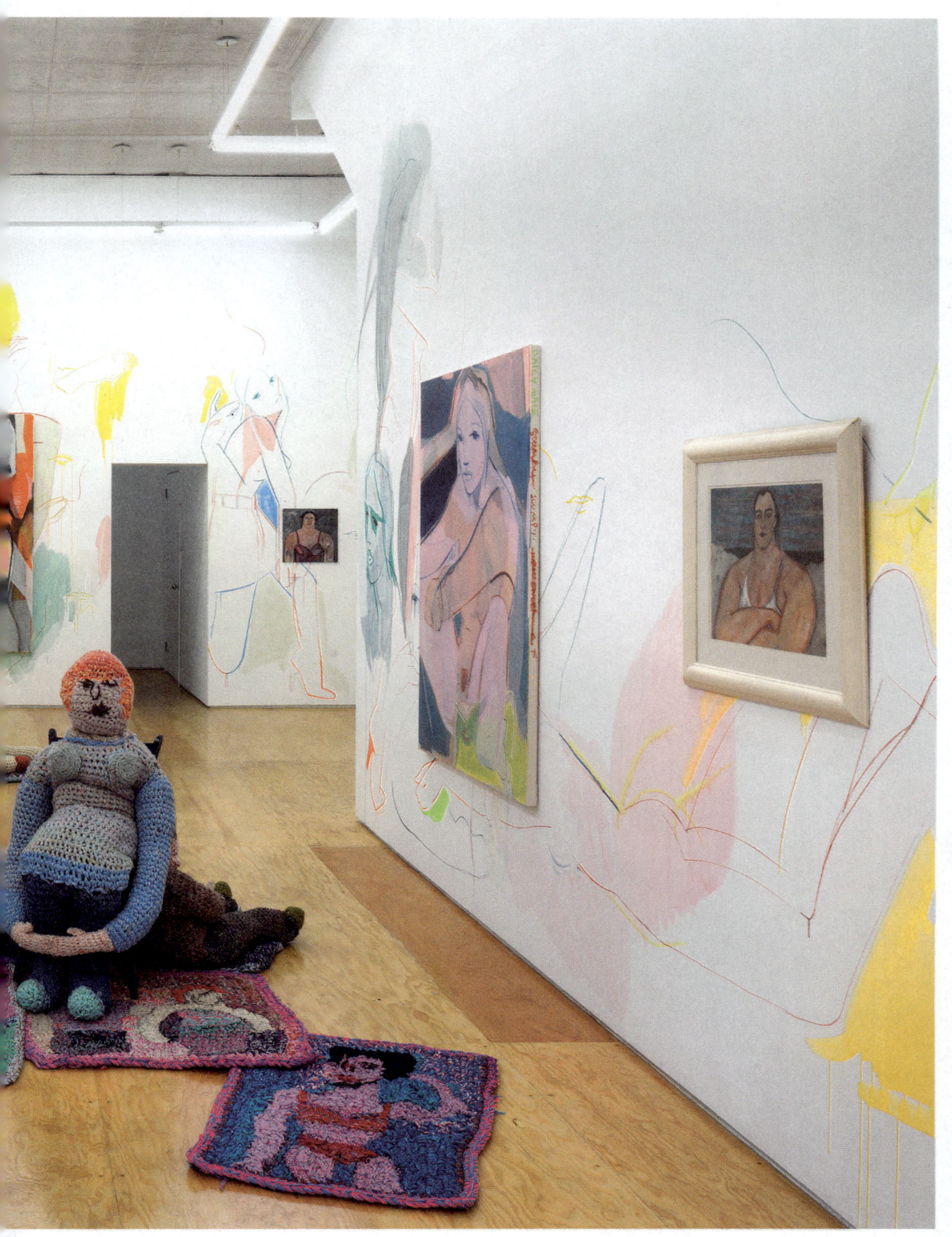

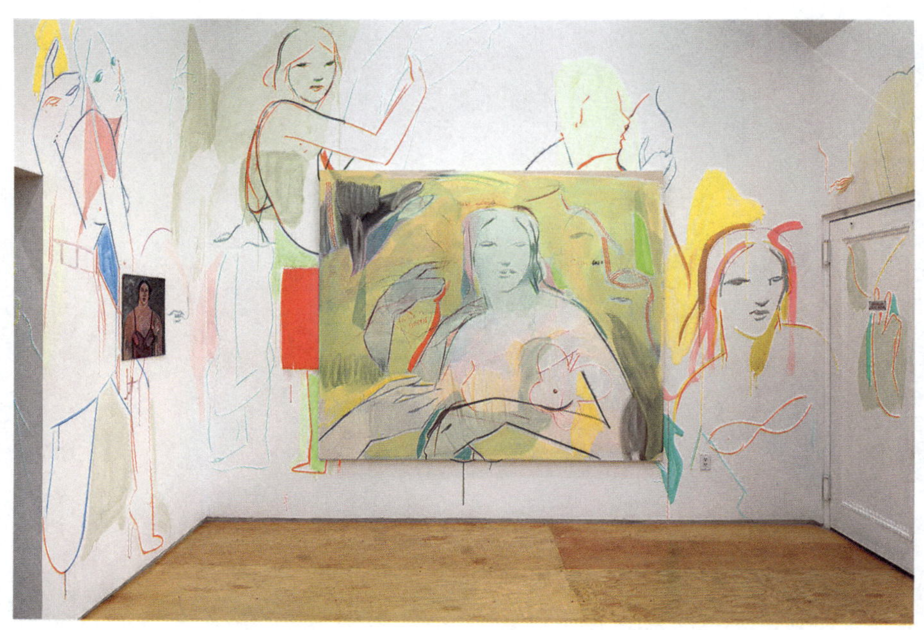

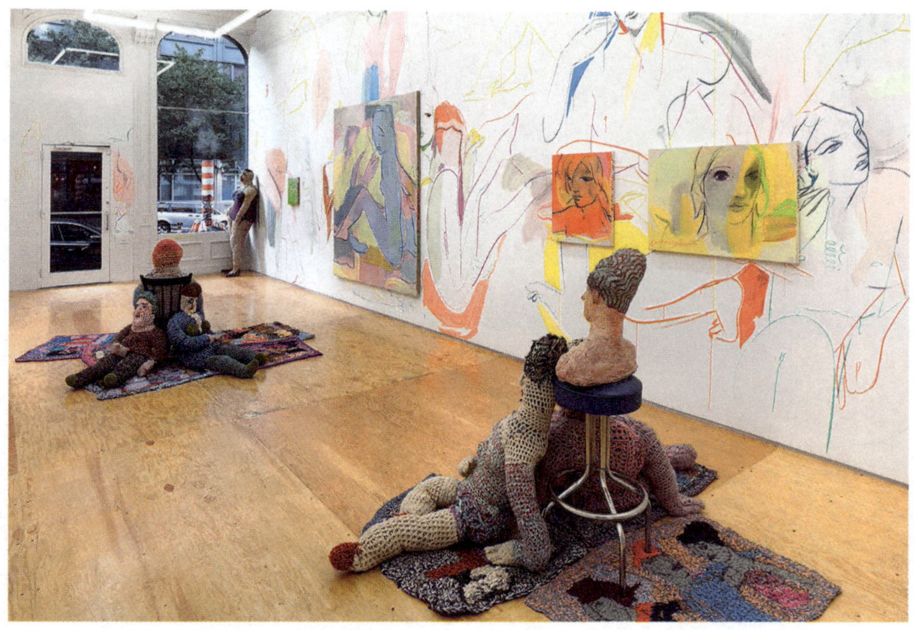

France-Lise McGurn and Rita McGurn. Matching Mother/Daughter Tattoos.
Exhibition view at Margot Samel, New York, September 2023.

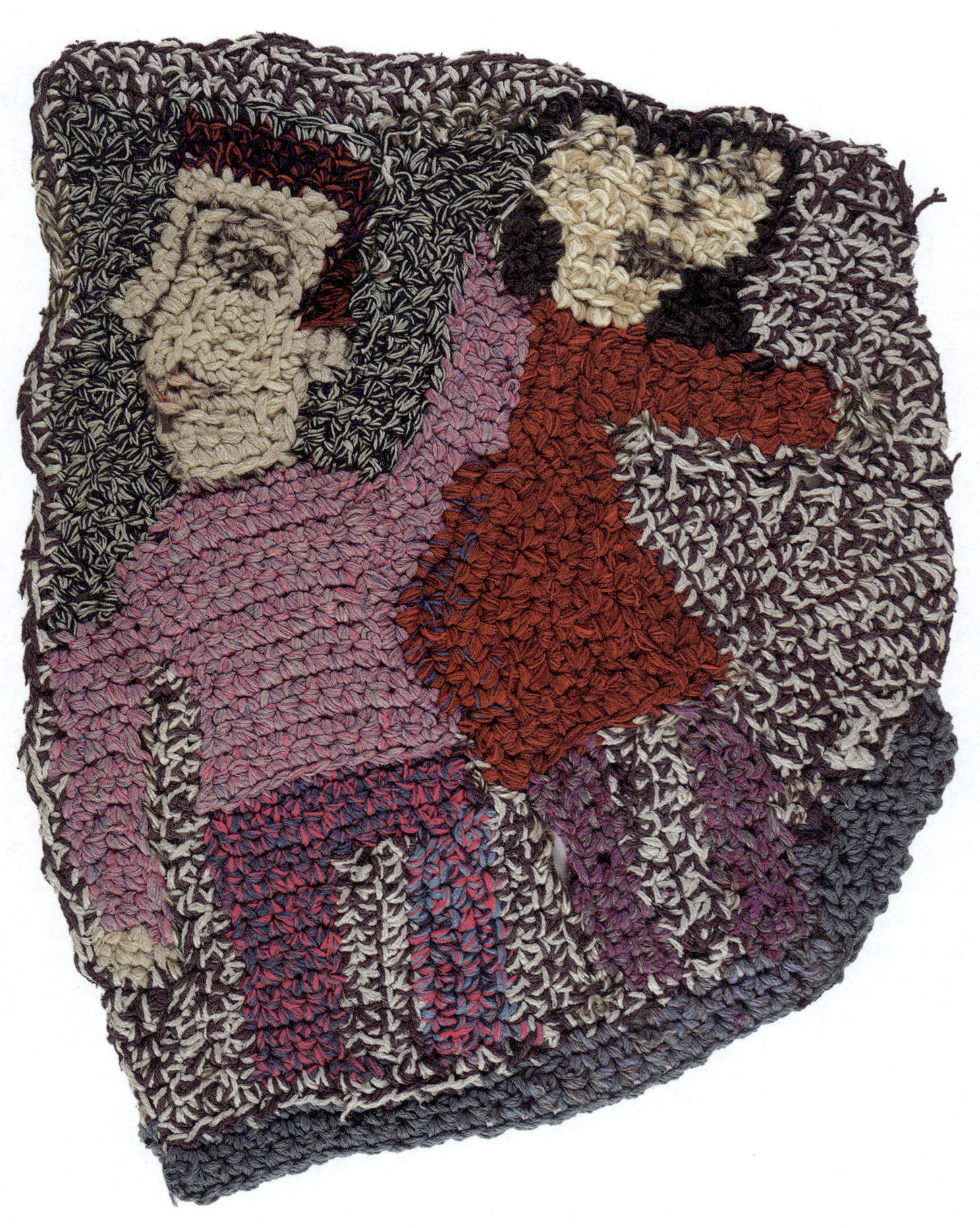

Rita McGurn. Untitled, 1990–2010

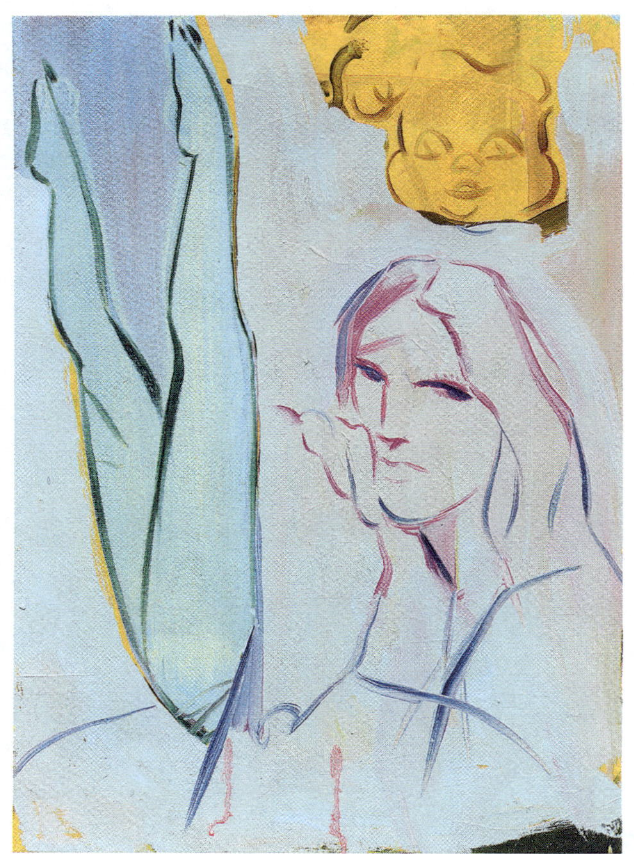

France-Lise McGurn. Cafe crème, 2023

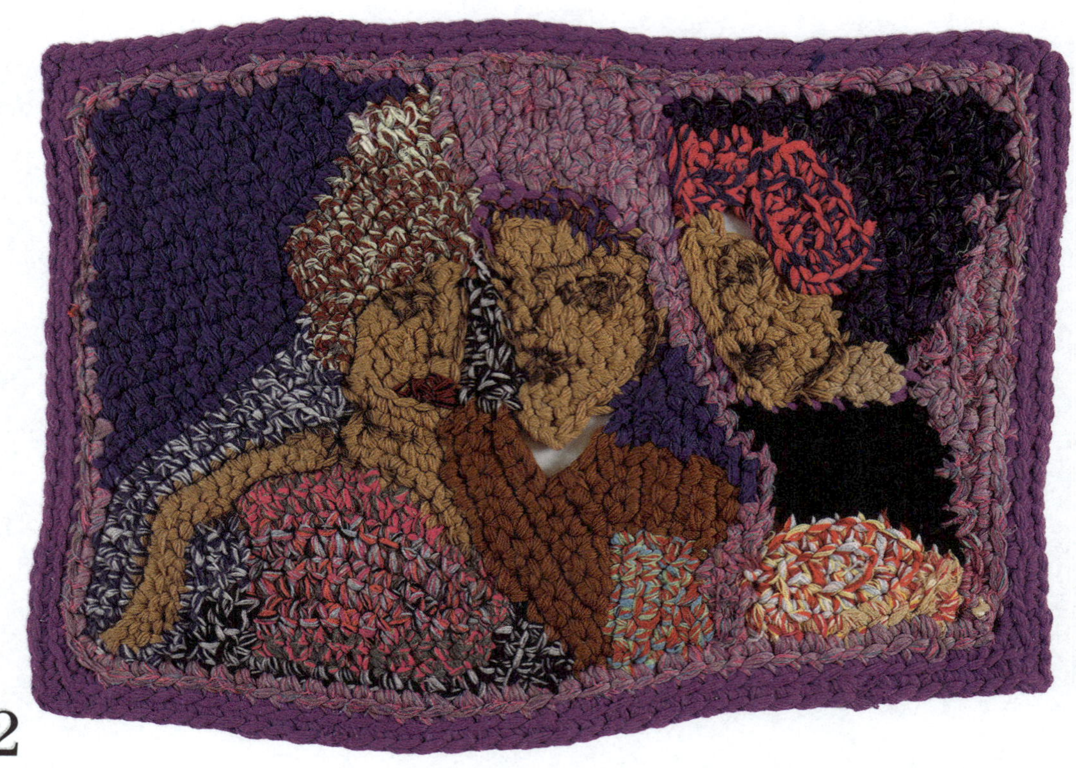

Rita McGurn. Untitled. 1990–2010

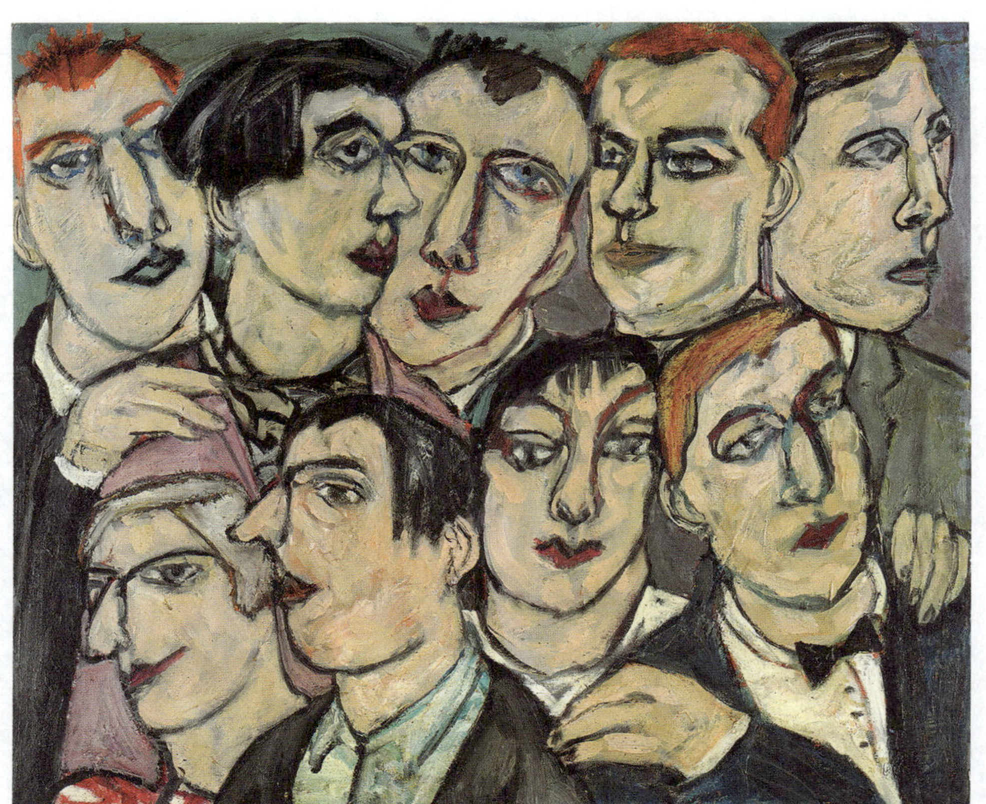

Rita McGurn. Untitled, 1990–1999

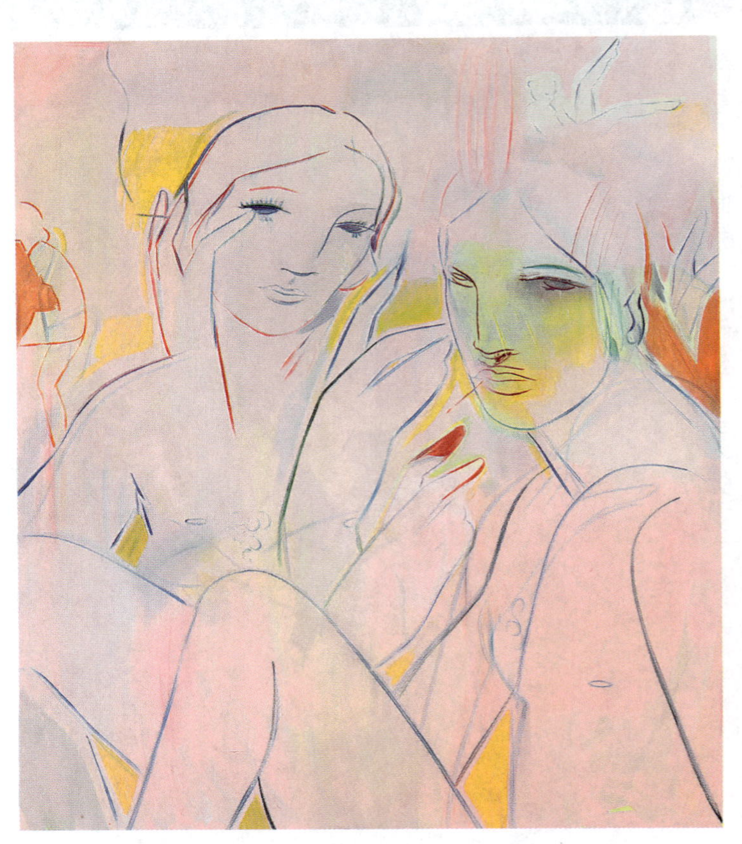

France-Lise McGurn. 80s mirror. 2023

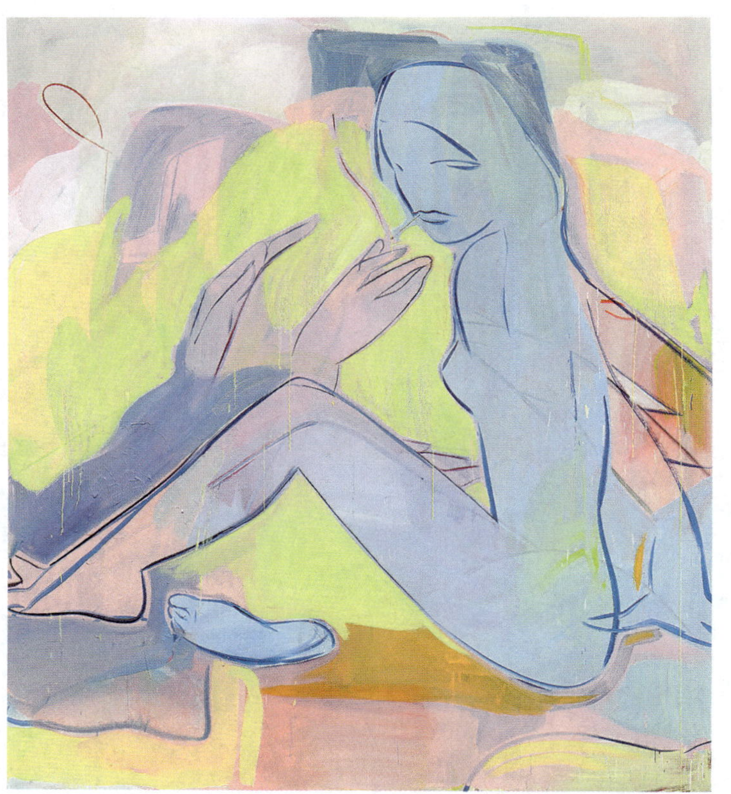

France-Lise McGurn. On fire, Joan of Arc, 2023

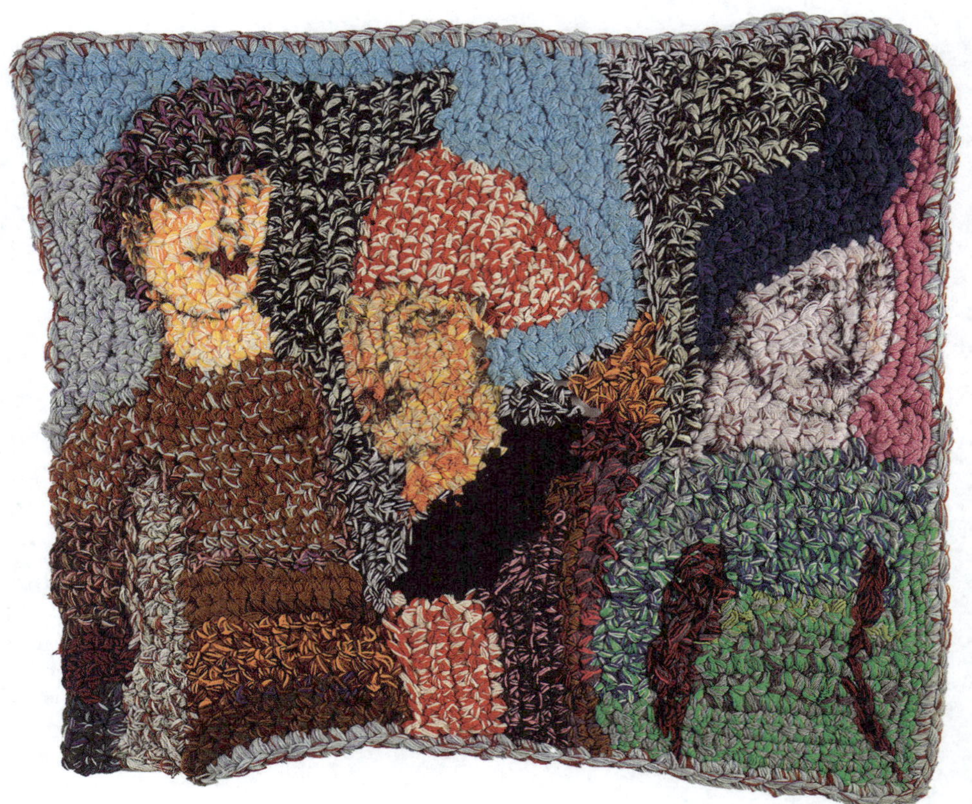

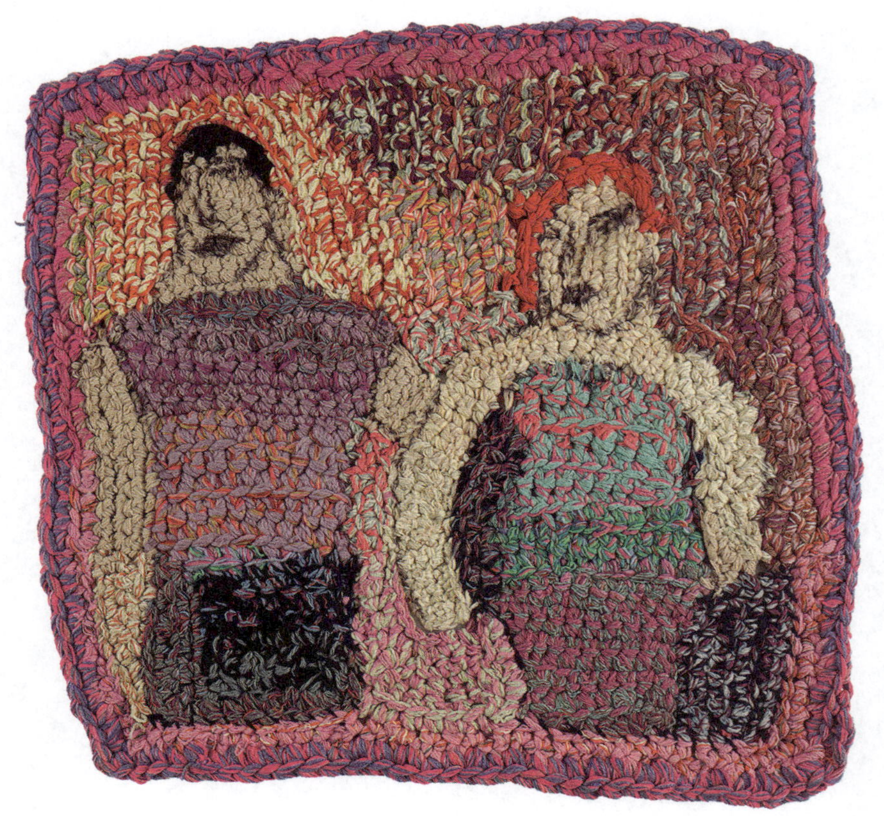

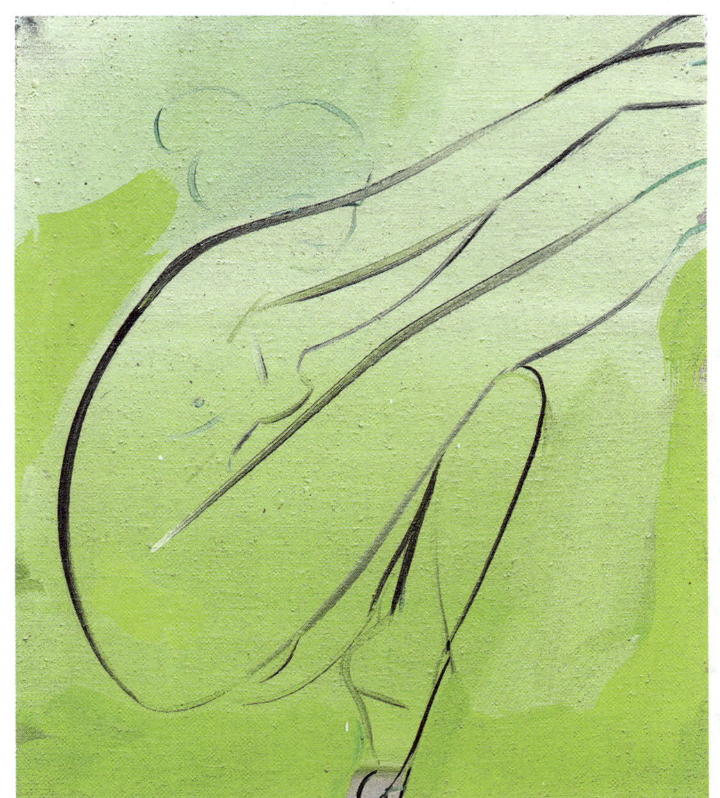

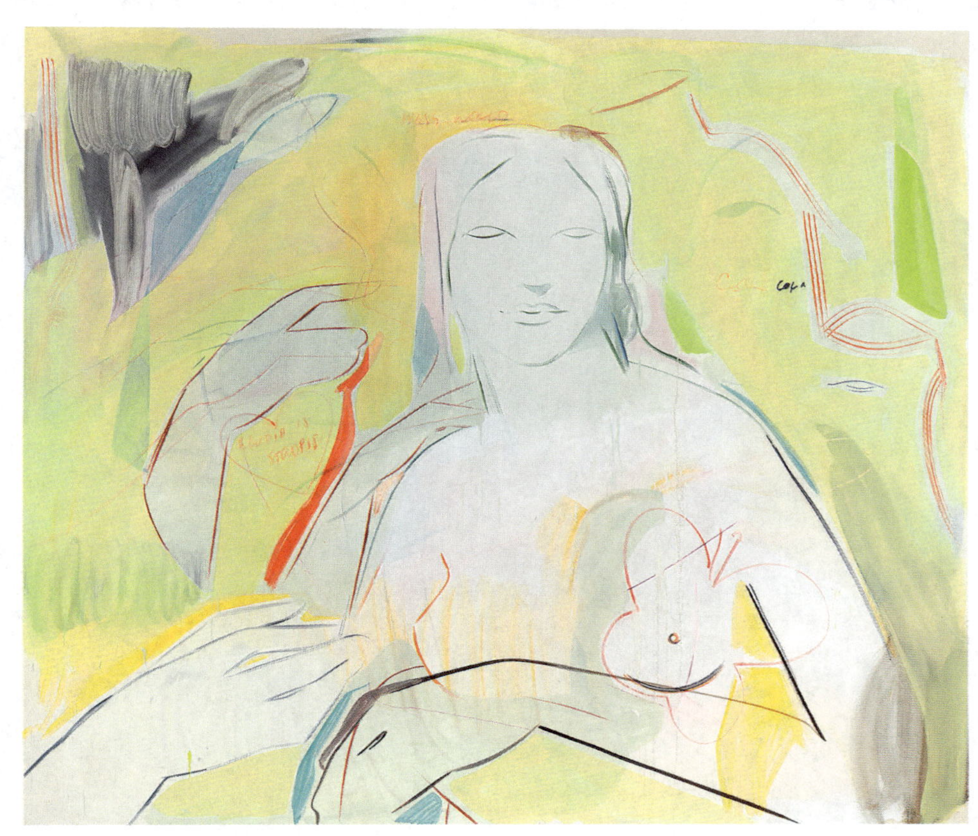

France-Lise McGurn. Pure classic, 2023

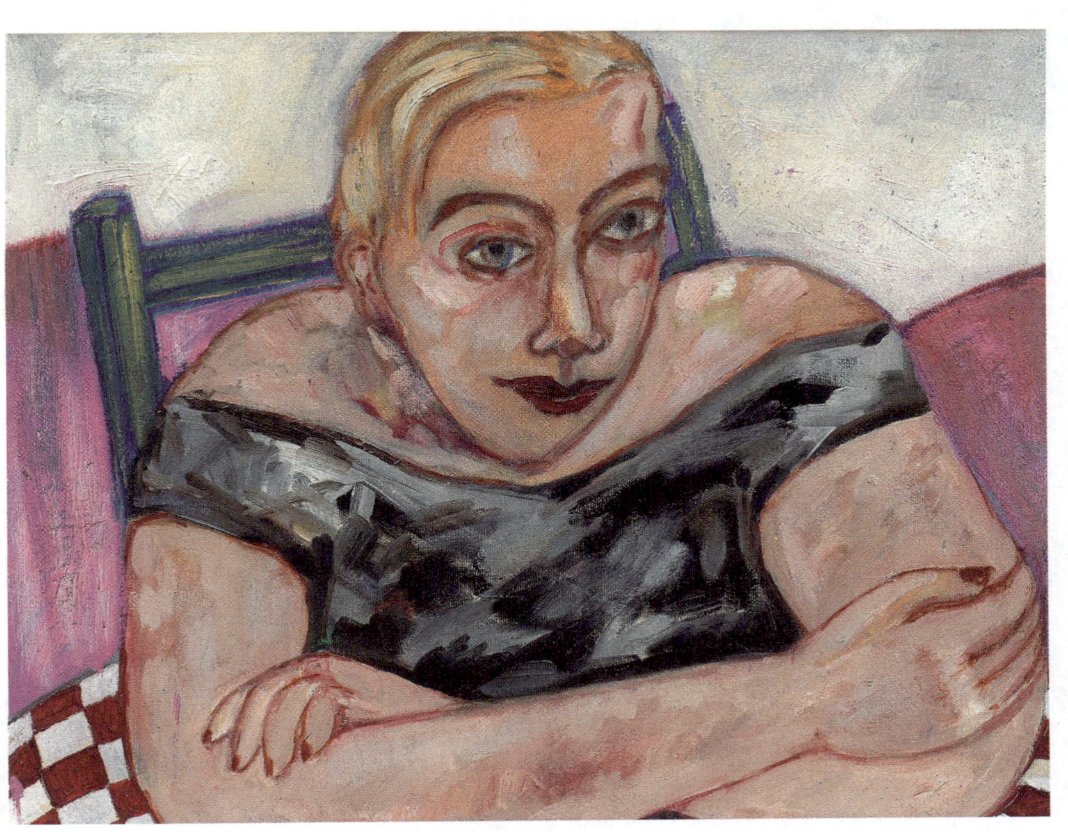

Rita McGurn. Untitled. 1990–1999

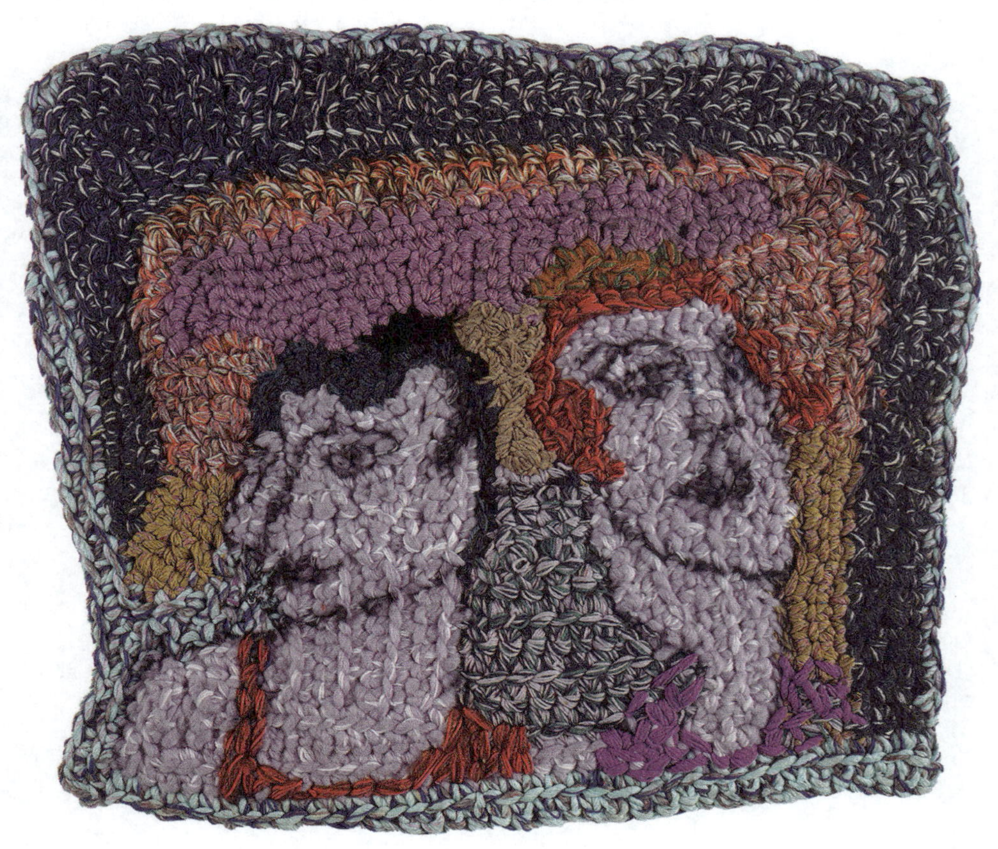

Rita McGurn. Untitled, 1990–2010

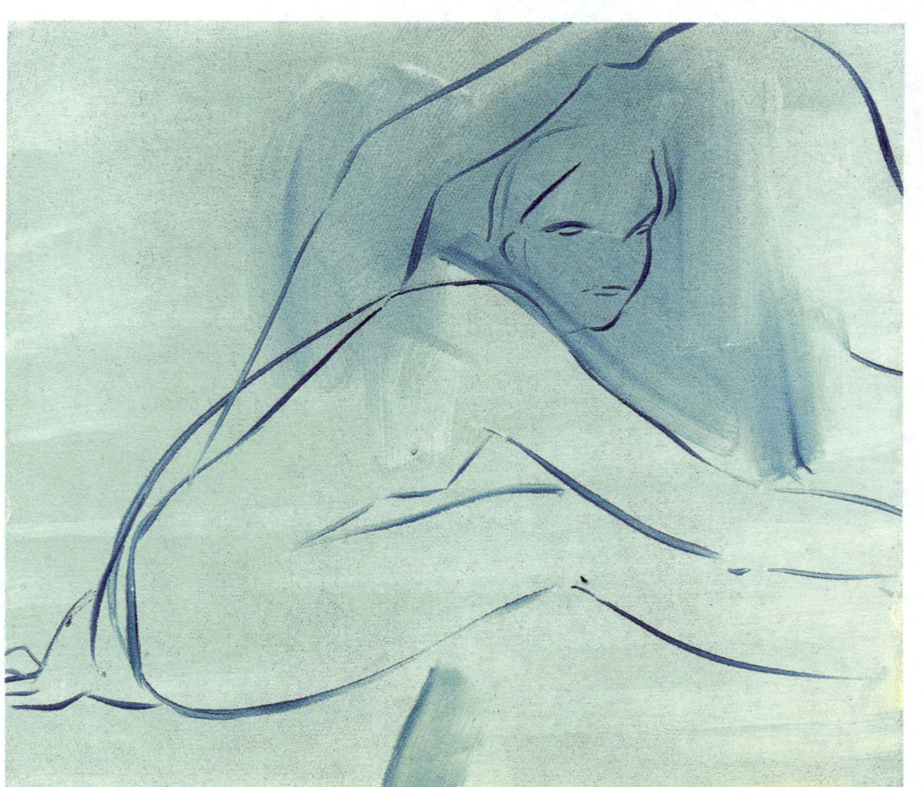

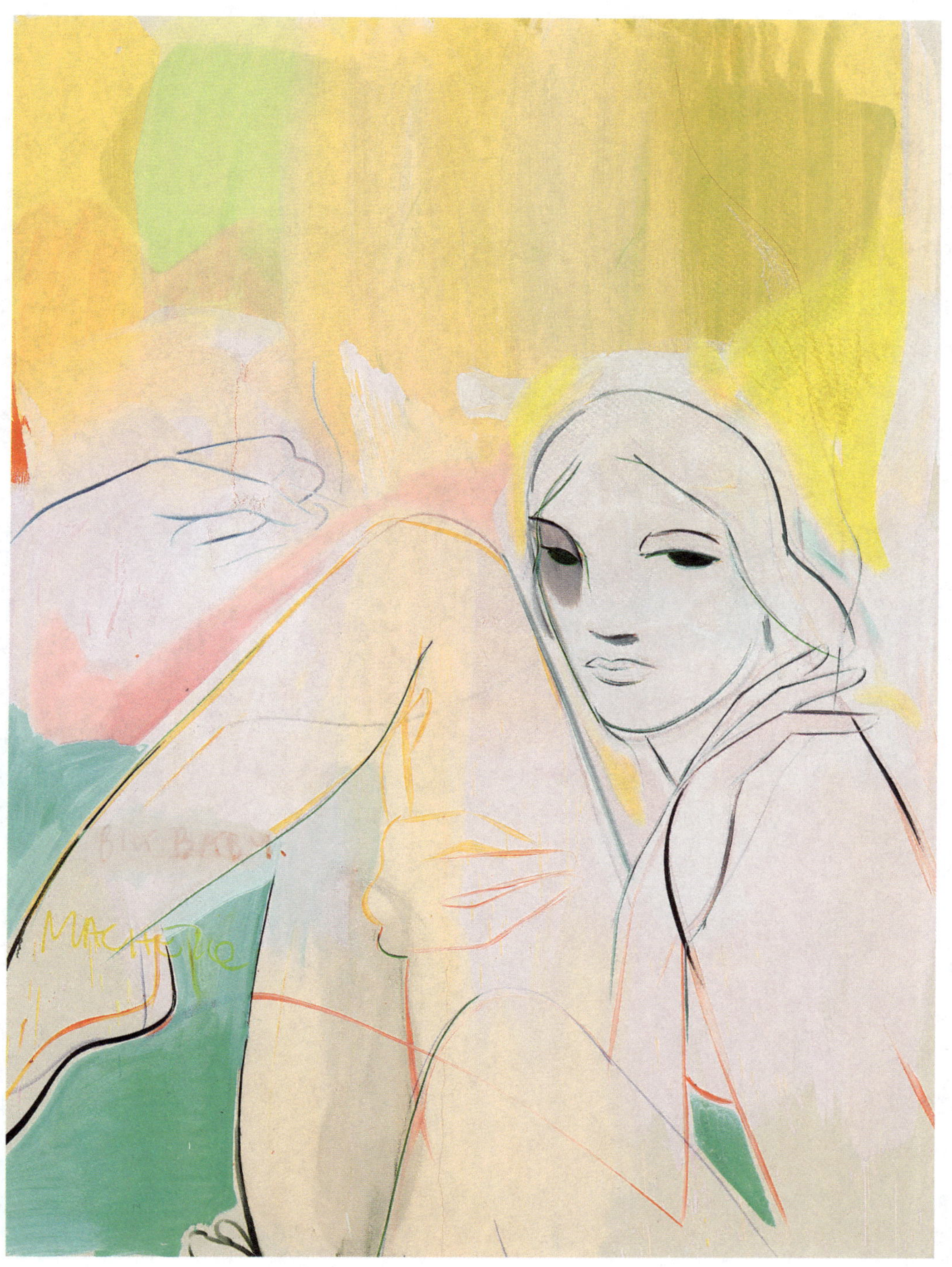

7
ta McGurn
ntitled, 2000–2010
ol
1/2 × 25 1/2 × 14 in

9
ance-Lise McGurn
mfluencer, 2023
and marker on linen
3/4 × 15 3/4 in

10
ta McGurn
ntitled, 1990–2010
ool and permanent marker
3/8 × 32 1/4 in

11
ta McGurn
ntitled, 1990–2010
ool and permanent marker
5/8 × 43 1/4 in

12
ance-Lise McGurn
s mirror, 2023
and marker on canvas
3/4 × 70 7/8 in

13
ance-Lise McGurn
ece peace, 2023
l and marker on canvas
5/8 × 27 1/2 in

14
ta McGurn
ntitled, 1990–1999
l on board
× 19 in (unframed)

15
ta McGurn
ntitled, 1990–2010
ool and permanent marker
1/2 × 42 1/2 in

16
ance-Lise McGurn
usic video, 2023
l and marker on canvas
1/2 × 23 5/8 in

p. 17
France-Lise McGurn
Sinéad, 2023
Oil and marker on canvas
27 1/2 × 39 3/8 in

p. 18
Rita McGurn
Untitled, 1990–1999
Oil on board
18 × 18 1/4 in

p. 20
France-Lise McGurn
Zoflora, the midnight blooms, 2023
Oil and marker on canvas
63 × 47 1/4 in

p.29
Rita McGurn
Untitled, 1990–2010
Wool and permanent marker
39 3/8 × 32 1/4 in

p. 31
France-Lise McGurn
Cafe crème, 2023
Oil and marker on linen
21 5/8 × 15 3/4 in

p. 32
Rita McGurn
Untitled, 1990–2010
Wool and permanent marker
29 7/8 × 42 1/2 in

p. 33
Rita McGurn
Untitled, 1990–1999
Oil on board
24 1/2 × 30 in

p. 34
France-Lise McGurn
80s mirror, 2023
Oil and marker on canvas
78 3/4 × 70 7/8 in

p. 35
France-Lise McGurn
On fire, Joan of Arc, 2023
Oil and marker on linen
86 5/8 × 78 3/4 in

p. 36
Rita McGurn
Untitled, 1990–2010
Wool and flecked glitter wool
39 3/8 × 49 1/4 in

p. 37
Rita McGurn
Untitled, 1990–2010
Wool and permanent marker
35 3/8 × 34 5/8 in

p. 38
France-Lise McGurn
Swinger, 2023
Oil and marker on linen
15 3/4 × 13 3/4 in

p. 39
France-Lise McGurn
Pure classic, 2023
Oil and marker on canvas
78 3/4 × 94 1/2 in

p. 40
Rita McGurn
Untitled, 1990–1999
Oil on board
14 1/4 × 19 in (unframed)

p. 41
Rita McGurn
Untitled, 1990–2010
Wool and unknown strand
31 1/2 × 34 1/4 in

p. 42
France-Lise McGurn
Guardian soul mates rip, 2023
Oil and marker on canvas
23 5/8 × 27 1/2 in

p. 43
France-Lise McGurn
Airhead, 2023
Oil and marker on canvas
63 × 47 1/4 in

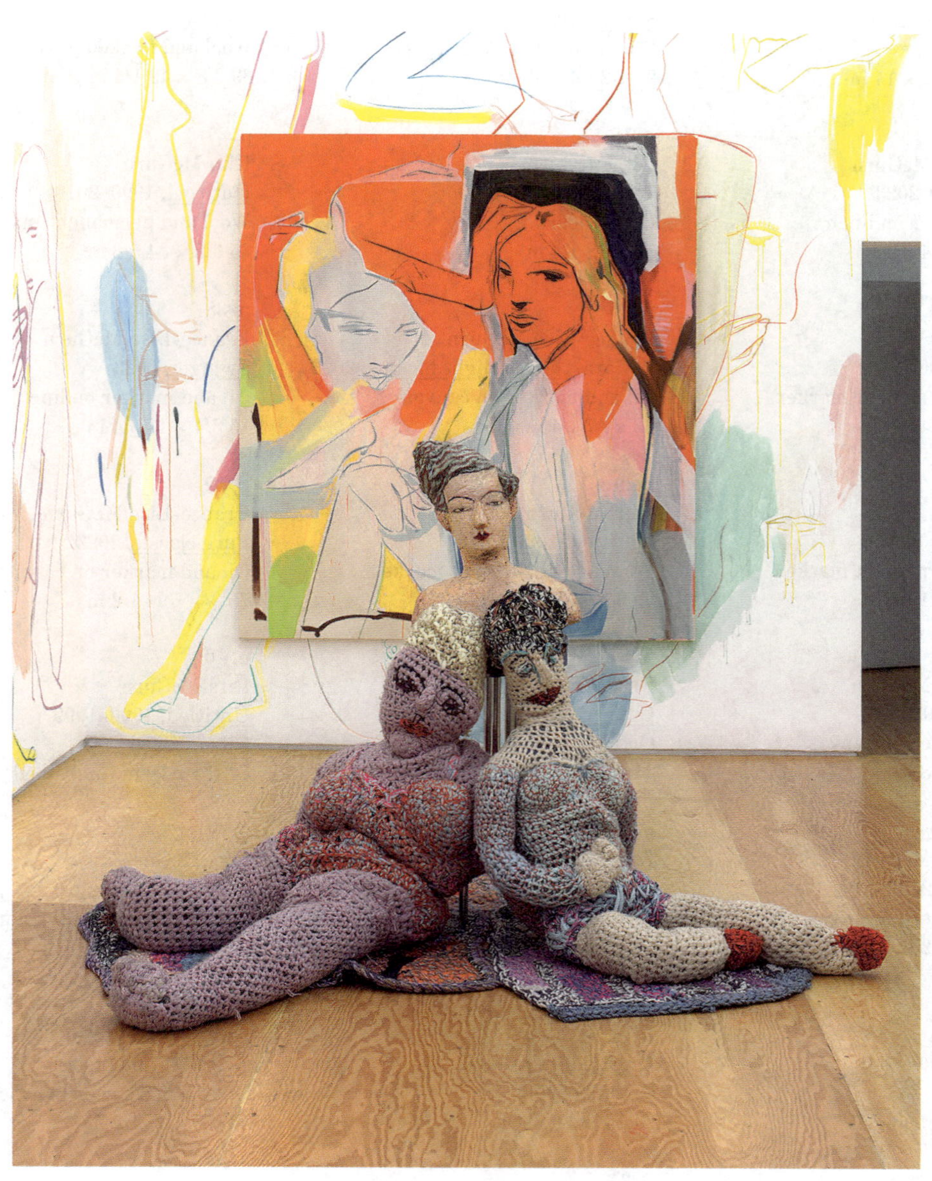

France-Lise McGurn and Rita McGurn. Matching Mother/Daughter Tattoos.
Exhibition view at Margot Samel, New York, September 2023.

RITA MCGURN (1940–2015, Glasgow, UK) was an artist and set designer who worked with figuration, painting, and textiles. Solo and two-person exhibitions include: Matching Mother/Daughter Tattoos, Margot Samel, New York, NY (2023); Rita McGurn, Gallery Celine, Glasgow, UK (2017); Gee-i-Ota, Rita McGurn Live!, iota, Glasgow, UK (2015); Rita McGurn: Off the Hook, Virginia Court, Glasgow, UK (2011), and at Todd Loft Building, Glasgow, UK (2004), and Compass Gallery, Glasgow, UK (1983). She is included in the upcoming exhibition Women in Revolt! Art, Activism and the Women's Movement in the UK 1970–1990, curated by Linsey Young, Zuzana Flaskova, Hannah Marsh, and Inga Fraser at Tate Britain, London, UK (2023).

FRANCE-LISE MCGURN (b. 1983, Glasgow, UK) is based in London, UK. She received a BFA in Painting from Duncan of Jordanstone College of Art, Dundee, UK (2005) and a MA in Painting from the Royal College of Art in London, UK (2012). Selected solo and two-person exhibitions include: Matching Mother/Daughter Tattoos, Margot Samel, New York, NY (2023); House Of Voltaire Presents France-Lise McGurn, Studio Voltaire, London, UK (2023); Aloud, The Exposé, Simon Lee Gallery, London, UK (2023); Aloud, The Exposé, at Simon Lee Gallery, London, UK (2022); Aloud, commission for Glasgow International, Kelvingrove Art Gallery and Museum, Glasgow, UK (2021); Percussia, Simon Lee Gallery, London, UK (2020); In Emotia, Tramway, Glasgow, UK (2020); Bodytronic, Kunsthaus Pasquart, Biel, Switzerland (2020); Art Now: France-Lise McGurn, Sleepless, Tate Britain, London, UK (2019); 0141, Frutta Gallery, Glasgow, UK (2018); Solo, Recent Activity Gallery, Birmingham, UK (2017); Archaos, Alison Jacques Gallery, London, UK (2017); France-Lise McGurn and Matthew Musgrave, Supplement Gallery, London, UK (2016); and 3am, Satellites Programme, Collective Gallery, Edinburgh, UK (2015). Select group exhibitions include Mark Making: Perspectives on Drawing, Gallery of Modern Art, Glasgow, UK; Body en Thrall, Rugby Art Gallery and Museum, Rugby, UK (2022); Drawing Biennial 2021, Drawing Room, London, UK (2021); New Arrivals: From Salvador Dali to Jenny Saville, Scottish National Gallery of Modern Art, Edinburgh, UK (2021); My Kid Could've Done That, The Edge, Bath, UK (2021); Mark Making: Perspectives on Drawing, Gallery of Modern Art, Glasgow, UK (2019); A Weakness for Raisins, CCA, Glasgow, UK (2018); Foundation Painting Show, Glasgow International, British Heart Foundation, Glasgow, UK (2018); Virginia Woolf: An Exhibition Inspired By Her Writings, Tate St. Ives, St. Ives, UK (2018, this exhibition travelled to Pallant House Gallery, Chichester, UK and The Fitzwilliam Museum, Cambridge, UK); Wall-Sun-Sun, Une Une Une, Perpignan, France (2017); (X)A Fantasy, David Roberts Art Foundation, London, UK (2017); Le Nouveau Voyeurisme, Hotel Contemporary, Milan, Italy (2017); Radical Vulnerability, Caustic Coastal, Manchester, UK (2016); The Old Things, Galerie Crevecoeur, Paris, France (2016); Home Salon, Marcelle Joseph Projects, Ascot, UK (2016) NEO-PAGAN BITCH-WITCH!, Evelyn Yard, London, UK (2016); Only With A Light Touch Will You Write Well, Freely and Fast, David Dale Gallery, Glasgow, UK (2015); Sexting, Kate Werble Gallery, New York, NY (2015); The Old Things, Galerie Crevecoeur, Paris, France (2015). Her work is in the public collections of Tate; Scottish National Gallery; Gallery of Modern Art (GoMA); Murray Edwards College; University of Cambridge; Hill Art Foundation; Dallas Museum of Art; K11 Art Foundation; Stiftung Kunsthaus-Sammlung Pasquart; The David and Indrė Roberts Collection; and New Hall Art Collection.

Published on the occasion of the exhibition

Matching Mother/Daughter Tattoos
France-Lise McGurn and Rita McGurn

at Margot Samel, 295 Church Street, New York
September 5 – October 14, 2023.

Text by Neil Clements
Designed by Indrek Sirkel

Photos by
Peter McGurn (p. 2)
Morwenna Grace (p. 4 bottom)
Lance Brewer (pp. 7, 10, 11, 14, 15, 18, 22–25, 27, 29, 32–33, 36–37, 40–41, 46)
Ollie Hammick (pp. 9, 12, 13, 16, 17, 20, 34–35, 38–39, 42–43)
Keith Hunter (p. 31)

France-Lise McGurn and Margot Samel would like to thank:
Patrick McAlindon, Lisette May Monroe, Louise Wright, Neil Clements, Linsey Young, Emily Small, Sharon Tawil, Indrek Sirkel, August Krogan-Roley, and the McGurn family

Published by Lugemik & Margot Samel

margotsamel.com
lugemik.com

ISBN 978-9916-9817-5-7

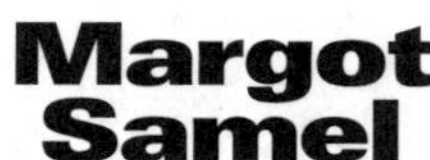